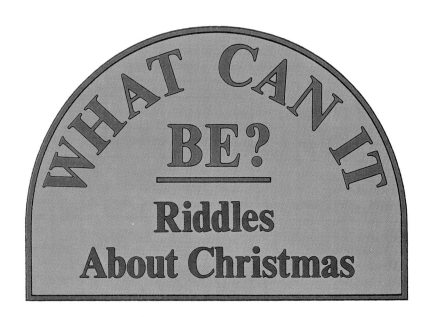

# WHAT CAN IT BE?

## Riddles About Christmas

By Jill Ashley

Photographs by Rob Gray

Silver Press

Published by Silver Press, a division of
Silver Burdett Press, Inc.
Simon & Schuster, Inc.
Prentice Hall Bldg., Englewood Cliffs, NJ 07632.

Printed in the United States of America.

Library of Congress Cataloging-in-Publication Data
Ashley, Jill
Riddles about Christmas
Jill Ashley; photos by Rob Gray.
p.    cm.——(What can it be?)
Summary: A collection of rhyming riddles describing various
aspects of Christmas and its celebration.
1. Riddles, Juvenile.   2. Christmas——Juvenile poetry.
[1. Christmas.   2. Riddles.]
I. Ashley, Jill   II. Gray, Rob. 1952–    [1].   III. Title.
IV. Series: Ball, Jacqueline A., What can it be?
PN6371.5.B23   1990      818'.5402——dc20
ISBN 0–671–70552–0 (lib. bdg.)                    90–8331
ISBN 0–671–70554–7                          CIP    AC

WHAT CAN IT BE? concept created by Jacqueline A. Ball.
For Jacqueline A. Ball Associates, Inc.:
J. A. Ball, President
Ann Hardy, Project Editor
Nancy Norton, Design Consultant
*What Can It Be: Riddles About Christmas*
edited by Susan Cornell Poskanzer

I'm covered with needles,
but still cannot sew.
I'm pointy on top,
round and wide down below.
I start out all green,
then I'm wrapped head to toe
with ribbons, and tinsel,
and bright lights that glow.

What am I?

## A CHRISTMAS TREE

Christmas celebrates the birth of Jesus Christ. It is a time of joy for Christians around the world. The Christmas tree has become one symbol of the holiday. Bringing a tree inside for Christmas began in Germany. The green trees remind people that in a few months spring will come again.

Clustered on clouds
while resting our wings,
we play lovely trumpets;
we strum on harp strings.
Some people put us
on top of their tree.
We're happy to be there.
We're quite heavenly.

What are we?

## ANGELS

According to the Bible, an angel told shepherds in the fields that Jesus was born in Bethlehem. Then the shepherds went into the village to see the Baby Jesus. Some people place an angel at the top of their Christmas tree.

We're diamond dots of scattered light,
like freckles on the face of night.

What are we?

# STARS

The Wise Men followed a star to find Jesus when he was born in a stable in Bethlehem. For this reason, many people top their Christmas tree with a star.

Some call me Father Christmas;
I'm round and always jolly.
I show up every winter,
when your halls are decked with holly.
I carry many presents,
stacked high inside my sleigh;
I have a team of reindeer
to guide me on my way.

Who am I?

# SANTA CLAUS

The idea of Santa Claus grew from stories about Saint Nicholas who gave gifts to needy people. Long ago children pictured Santa as a tall, thin man who wore church robes and rode a great white horse. In Hawaii, Santa Claus doesn't drive a sleigh. He comes by boat!

We hang near the fire, empty at first.
We wait for a man in a sleigh.
He fills us with toys
for good girls and boys,
then merrily goes on his way.

What are we?

# CHRISTMAS STOCKINGS

The idea of hanging Christmas stockings near the fire probably began with Dutch settlers around New Amsterdam. Washington Irving first wrote about a fat Santa Claus who filled children's stockings with small presents and treats.

I'm sort of a wagon,
without any wheel,
I glide over snow
with my runners of steel.
I don't have a motor
or engine that moves,
I'm powered by pairs
of proud prancing hooves.

What am I?

## A SLEIGH

Sleighs have runners that glide easily over ice and snow. In some cold places, sleighs are used for everyday transportation. They are often pulled by horses or reindeer.

Made of silver,
made of steel,
we can jingle, clang, and peal.
We can jangle.
We can chime.
We ring out at Christmas time.

What are we?

## BELLS

Many bells ring at Christmas time. Church bells call people to worship and sing hymns. Doorbells tell that company has arrived. People in stores and on streets ring handbells as they collect money for charity.

We sing your favorite Christmas songs.
We keep your spirits bright.
We go all through the neighborhood.
Our music fills the night.
Our songs are truly beautiful.
They tell the Christmas story.
We're glad to share fine tunes that sing
of Christmas joy and glory.

What are we?

## CAROLERS

At one time, some Christmas carols were not considered religious enough to sing inside the churches. Since people loved the songs, carolers sang them outside instead. Today grateful listeners still give carolers warm drinks as thanks for the holiday entertainment.

Hanging on your Christmas door,
I'm such a welcome sight.
I'm made of branches, twigs, and things
that shine and sparkle bright.
I sometimes grace a room or hall
to please all those who enter.
Choose any lovely Christmas spot
and place me in the center.

What am I?

# A WREATH

Some people believe that wreaths represent the crown of thorns Jesus wore in Jerusalem. Early wreaths were simple green branches. Today beautiful wreaths, made of everything from flowers and herbs to candies, welcome Christmas guests.

We may be even better
for you to GIVE than get.
We rest beneath the Christmas tree.
We're often bought and yet . . .
you sometimes make us with your hands.
You paint, or bake, or sew;
then wrap us in a fancy box,
and tie us with a bow.

What are we?

# PRESENTS

People give gifts on Christmas, just as the Wise Men gave precious gold and perfumes to the Baby Jesus. Homemade gifts are wonderful because they take extra care and thought. Many people also give gifts to charity. This special giving shows the true spirit of Christmas.

I've leaves as red
as ripest cherries.
At my center,
yellow berries.
I add dash
to Christmas scenery—
ruby splashes
in the greenery.

What am I?

# A RED POINSETTIA PLANT

The bright red leaves of poinsettia plants make them a favorite decoration at Christmas time. The plant was named after Dr. Joel Poinsett, who first brought the plant to the United States in the 1800s.

Each year at Christmas,
I'm such a sweet treat,
a swirl of mint flavors,
you can't wait to eat.
I hook on your tree branch.
I'm thin or I'm thick.
Just tear off my wrapper,
and give me a lick.

What am I?

## A CANDY CANE

Candy canes often look like shepherd's crooks. According to the Bible, shepherds saw angels in the sky when Jesus was born. Today red and white candy canes are a favorite Christmas sweet.

I have a jaw that can be shut
upon the shell of any nut.
If you press hard, I crack and crunch,
then give you back a snack to munch.

What am I?

# A NUTCRACKER

*The Nutcracker Suite* is a famous ballet. It tells about a girl and her favorite Christmas toy, a nutcracker that looks like a soldier. She dreams that the nutcracker comes to life and saves her from evil mice. Later the nutcracker becomes a handsome prince. The ballet is often performed at Christmas time.

We look like real people,
although we are not.
Sometimes we're cold.
Sometimes we're hot.
Frosting and raisins
in just the right places
put jolly smiles
on all of our faces.

What are we?

## GINGERBREAD PEOPLE

Long ago in England, bakers made little people from scraps of bread dough and called them Johnny Boys. Later, they added ginger and molasses to create the gingerbread cookies we enjoy at Christmas time today.

A teddy bear to take to bed,
a ball, a bike,
a sleek new sled.
A train that moves around a track,
a doll that talks,
bright blocks to stack.
We're many things a child enjoys.
Come play with us,
for we are ____.

What are we?

## TOYS

Toys are favorite
Christmas gifts
of children all
over the world.
Today many
people collect
toys to give to
needy children
at Christmas
time. Sharing
makes everyone
feel good during
the holiday
season.